Dramasc

Crimes and Punishments

Lad Carl

The Testing of Tseng

The Question

Three traditional tales dramatised by
JOHN O'CONNOR
with explanatory notes and activities

Nelson

Nelson
Nelson House
Mayfield Road
Walton-on-Thames
Surrey KT12 5PL
United Kingdom

Copyright © Scripts: John O'Connor 2000

The right of John O'Connor to be identified as author of these plays has been asserted by John O'Connor in accordance with the Copyright, Design and Patents Act 1988. All applications to perform any of these plays should be addressed in the first instance to the Royalty and Permissions Department, ITPS Ltd, Cheriton House, North Way, Andover, Hampshire SP10 5BE (Tel 01264 342756; Fax 01264 342792).

Introduction, activities, explanatory notes and illustrations
Copyright © Nelson 2000

Project management by Elizabeth Paren
Designed and formatted by Geoffrey Wadsley
Art editing by Jane Taylor
Edited by Alison Hart
Cover illustration by Dave Grimwood, Pelican Graphics
Black and white illustrations by Gerry Grace (*Lad Carl*) and Pat Moffett (*Testing of Tseng* and *The Question*)
Printed by L. Rex Printing Co. Ltd, China

This edition first published by Nelson 2000
ISBN 0-17-432617-3
9 8 7 6 5 4 3 2 1
03   02   01   00

All rights reserved. No part of this publication may be reproduced, copied or transmitted in any form or by any means, electronic or mechanical, including photocopy, recording, or any information storage and retrieval system, without permission in writing from the publisher or under license from the Copyright Licensing Authority Ltd., 90 Tottenham Court Road, London W1P 9HE.

Contents

Series Editor's Introduction — IV
Worldwide Dramascripts — V
Introduction — VI

Lad Carl — 1
Where the Tale Comes From — 3
The Characters — 4
The Play — 5

The Testing of Tseng — 25
Where the Tale Comes From — 27
The Characters — 28
The Play — 29

The Question — 63
Where the Tale Comes From — 65
The Characters — 66
The Play — 67

Looking Back at the Plays — 89

INTRODUCTION

Series Editor's Introduction

Dramascripts is an exciting series of plays especially chosen for students in the lower and middle years of secondary school. The titles range from the best in modern writing to adaptations of classic texts such as *A Christmas Carol* and *Silas Marner*.

Dramascripts can be read or acted purely for the enjoyment and stimulation that they provide; however, each play in the series also offers all the support that pupils need in working with the text in the classroom:

- **Introduction** – this offers important background information and explains something about the ways in which the play came to be written.
- **Script** – this is clearly set out in ways that make the play easy to handle in the classroom.
- **Notes** explain references that pupils might not understand, and language points that are not obvious.
- **Activities** – at the end of scenes, acts or sections – give pupils the opportunity to explore the play more fully. Types of activity include: discussion, writing, hot-seating, improvisation, acting, freeze-framing, story-boarding and artwork.
- **Looking Back at the Play** – this section has further activities for more extended work on the play as a whole, with emphasis on characters, plots, themes and language.

John O'Connor

WORLDWIDE DRAMASCRIPTS

Whether we look at the Caribbean or China, ancient India or medieval Europe, we find that cultures across the world and throughout history have had one fundamental thing in common: they have all created myths, legends and traditional tales, in an endeavour to make sense of their existence and to confront the most challenging issues of right and wrong.

Worldwide Dramascripts present some of the most exciting and intriguing examples of these tales in the form of lively and thought-provoking playscripts. These bring together figures such as Theseus and Rama, Anansi and Guinevere, Hanuman the monkey-god and the famous Lambton Worm.

With the exception of *Goat Song* – an original retelling of Greek myths in a single play – each anthology brings together three or four short plays with a connecting theme, raising questions about:
- right and wrong
- justice and retribution
- the nature of heroism
- the eternal tensions between brothers and sisters
- the joys and pain of love
- the never-ending need to escape.

Because they feature such basic human concerns the plays and activities in Worldwide Dramascripts offer opportunities for students to engage with issues of enduring significance while enjoying some of the greatest stories ever told.

John O'Connor

Introduction

These three plays are all based upon old folk tales from different parts of the world, and all throw fascinating lights on the ways in which different people through the ages have told stories in an attempt to explore the basic questions about law and judgement facing their cultures. For us today they raise – in a way that is both entertaining and thought-provoking – some of the most complex and challenging questions we are likely to have to face in dealing with wrongdoings:

- Should the punishment fit the crime?
- Is it important to devise punishments which help the wrongdoer to reform?
- How do we react to the different punishments that characters receive in stories?
- In catching criminals, do the ends justify the means?

Together these three plays offer a stimulating introduction to the continuing debate about crime and punishment.

John O'Connor

Dramascripts

Lad Carl

Dramatised by
JOHN O'CONNOR

WHERE THE TALE COMES FROM

Set against a background of mountain villages, howling wolves and remote forest cabins, *Lad Carl* is an old Scandinavian story about a young man's decision to catch the thieves who have been ravaging his homeland.

Joining the gang as a new recruit, Carl draws upon qualities of wit and cunning, as much as leadership and practicality, to bring about a dramatic and unexpected result. But his achievement raises some challenging questions . . .

NELSON DRAMASCRIPTS

THE CHARACTERS

The villagers

CARL *16 years old; known as 'Lad Carl'.*

GRETTIR *his mother.*

HALLBJORN *a farmer.*

VILLAGERS *

The thieves

THURID *their housekeeper.*

THORGAUT *their leader.*

GRIM

SKAPTI

JOKULL

* indicates non-speaking part

PRONOUNCING THE NAMES

GRETTIR *Gret-ear*

HALLBJORN *Hal-byorn*

THURID *Too-rid*

THORGAUT *Tor-gout*

SKAPTI *Scap-tee*

JOKULL *Yo-ckel*

Lad Carl

Scene 1

Early morning in winter. A courtyard of a peasant's cottage in a small village somewhere in Scandinavia, many centuries ago. GRETTIR is pumping water. Her son CARL enters from the house, stuffing clothes into a canvas bag, and carrying a wooden slatted box, inside which we hear a pigeon cooing.

GRETTIR	*(Looking up, but carrying on with her pumping.)* What do you mean, you're going to be a thief-catcher?	1
CARL	A thief-catcher. Catch thieves.	
GRETTIR	But it's not a career.	
CARL	I don't see why not. Harald's a dog-catcher. Sveinn catches fish. I'll be a thief-catcher.	
GRETTIR	You'll come to no good.	
CARL	I'll come to no good stuck here, mother. Look, I'll give it a try for a year. If it doesn't work out, I'll come home and get a job on the farm.	10
GRETTIR	But why do you have to go now? It's winter. There's no-one on the roads. You'll freeze before you get to town. At least stay till the spring.	
CARL	No. My mind's made up. If I don't go now, I'll be stuck here for ever. *(Picking up the box.)* Come on, pigeon.	
	(He walks off and turns to take a farewell look at the cottage.)	
	I'll write to you, I promise.	

GRETTIR Fat chance.

CARL Wish me luck.

GRETTIR Luck. *(As he leaves she calls after him.)* You'll need it. *(She picks up her full pail and goes off towards the house, stops and then calls out after him as the lights dim.)* And don't take the mountain road – it's infested with wolves!

The lights dim to the sound of wolves howling.

Scene 2

As the wolf howls die away, the lights come up on the interior of a mountain cabin. Apart from a table and some chairs, there are stuffed animals' heads on the walls, together with a collection of axes, pikes and guns and an old clock. A fire burns in the grate but it is partially obscured by a clothes horse covered in washing.

Outside the wind blows more powerfully than before. There is a knocking at the door. Then another. After a few seconds CARL enters, covered in snow. He looks around cautiously and, closing the door after him, strides over to the fire to warm himself.

CARL	(Calling out.) Hello. Anyone at home?	1
	(Receiving no reply, CARL takes his coat off and throws it over a chair. He sits down and is about to remove his boots when he hears a voice.)	
THURID	I wouldn't stay here if I were you.	
	(He looks around, but sees no-one.)	
CARL	Sorry?	
	(THURID, an old woman, appears from behind the clothes horse, where she has been sitting on a stool.)	
THURID	I said I wouldn't stay here if I were you. This is a thieves' lair, this is.	10
CARL	Ah, good evening, mother. I was wondering if I might have a bed for the night. It's bitter out there.	
THURID	A thieves' lair.	
CARL	Really? You wouldn't have anything hot to eat, I suppose? I can pay . . . though I haven't much.	
	(He pulls a small leather bag from inside his shirt, opens it and a single coin falls out on to the table. CARL regards	

SCENE 2

it apologetically; the old woman treats it with the disdain that it deserves.)

THURID Thieves. Violent, merciless and unscrupulous.

CARL *(As though they are three names he can't quite place.)* Don't think I've heard of them. Come to think of it, forget the food – I've a crust in my bag will keep me going. What I really need is a good sleep. Bedrooms up here, are they?

(And he picks up his luggage – the bag and the pigeon in its box – and ascends the stairs, while THURID, muttering away to herself, collects the washing from the clothes horse and folds it up.)

THURID . . . Unscrupulous, reckless and devil-may-care.

(As she works, we hear the sound of approaching horses, closely followed by men's voices, arguing. The door bursts open and the THIEVES enter, clearly in a bad mood.)

GRIM I told you it would be a waste of time. Who would be travelling on a day like this?

THORGAUT My information was . . .

GRIM Your information! It was your information that had us waiting three days for . . .

THORGAUT They were held up. I cannot be held responsible for . . .

GRIM You're supposed to be our leader, aren't you? Who else do we hold responsible? You're our *(Sarcastically.)* 'captain'.

 **unscrupulous** *Not caring how much harm they do.*

THORGAUT	Do you want the job?
GRIM	Well I couldn't make a worse . . .
	(He breaks off: SKAPTI has found CARL's coat.)
SKAPTI	*(To THURID.)* What's this?
THURID	Traveller. *(She nods over her shoulder and they all look up in the direction of the rooms upstairs, forgetting their arguments for a moment.)*
JOKULL	Any money?
	(She picks up the single coin from the table and shows it to them.)
THURID	Oh, and a pet pigeon.
SKAPTI	Does he know about us?
THURID	*(Nods.)* I told him: cunning, depraved and ruthless. *(Muttering as she leaves.)* Wouldn't listen, though.
JOKULL	What do we do?
GRIM	Throw him down the ravine.
SKAPTI	Feed him to the wolves.
JOKULL	Drown him.
GRIM	*(To THORGAUT.)* You're 'captain' – you decide.
	(But, before another argument can get under way, CARL's voice is heard from the top of the stairs.)

 **depraved** *Totally immoral.*

SCENE 2   NELSON DRAMASCRIPTS

CARL   Good evening. We haven't met, but my name is Carl. *(Calmly he descends and joins them.)* I think I must have another name, but I'm damned if I know what it is. Mother always calls me 'Lad Carl'. I was wondering – you wouldn't have a vacancy for a trainee thief, I suppose?   70

Blackout.

a vacancy *A job opportunity; an opening.*

ARTWORK: Draw two sketches of simple stage sets which could represent the courtyard in Scene 1 and the interior of the cabin in Scene 2. Try to create something which could serve for both scenes by some simple adaptation.

DISCUSSION: What have the thieves been up to before their entrance in Scene 2? What has made Grim so angry? What have you learned about the relationship between Grim and Thorgaut?

Scene 3

Later that night. When the lights go up we see that CARL is tied to a chair and gagged. The THIEVES are sitting around and look as though they have been discussing something for a long time.

JOKULL	Or drop boulders on to him from a great height.	1
SKAPTI	Eaten by bears. That's always plausible.	
THORGAUT	But what if he isn't a spy? What if . . .	
GRIM	Of course he's a spy. We are the notorious Shadowdale Gang – *(He rips a Wanted poster off the wall and reads.)* 'terrorisers of the border settlements'. Five times the farmers have sent out vigilantes to catch us and each time we have evaded them. We are cunning.	
THURID	Ruthless and devil-may-care.	10
GRIM	In their frustration the authorities have come to realise that their only chance to catch us is to infiltrate our operation.	
THORGAUT	He doesn't look like a spy.	
GRIM	What do you expect? A black hat and a cloak?	
THORGAUT	I mean he's skinny and underfed. He looks more like . . . well, a thief.	

vigilantes *Unofficial law enforcement groups.*

infiltrate our operation *(Criminal jargon.) Arrange for an undercover agent to join the gang and spy on them.*

SCENE 3

SKAPTI	Why don't we set him a test? A kind of trial. We give him a job to do. If he does it, he's in. If he fails, we kill him. Easy.
THORGAUT	What sort of trial?
SKAPTI	I have received information . . .
GRIM	Oh, not you as well!
THORGAUT	Shut up, Grim, and listen.
SKAPTI	I have received information that old Hallbjorn plans to take one of his oxen to market tomorrow. If Lad Carl here wants to prove he's genuine about becoming a thief, all he has to do is steal it.
	(There is a silence as they all mull this over.)
GRIM	I'm uneasy.
JOKULL	So what's the alternative?
THORGAUT	All right. See what he says.
	(They remove CARL's gag.)
	Did you hear all that?
CARL	Certainly. When do I start?
	Blackout.

Scene 4

It is dawn the next morning and the light comes up on a track through the mountain pass. The weather has improved and there is the sound of bird song. CARL enters from the right, jumps up on to a boulder and looks off behind him. After a second or two he hears the sound that he is waiting for: an ox bellowing. He jumps down from the rock, reaches into his bag and produces a colourfully decorated leather shoe, which he places carefully in the middle of the path. Checking once more that his man is on his way, CARL hides behind the boulder and waits.

HALLBJORN the farmer enters from left, pulling on a rope, which suddenly tightens, forcing him to an unexpected standstill. Not in the best of tempers – it is a long haul from his valley farm, over the mountains to market – he jerks angrily on the rope. The ox bellows offstage but nothing happens. HALLBJORN is about to go back and discipline the animal when he notices the shoe.

SCENE 4

HALLBJORN Hello! What a very handsome shoe.

(He picks it up and examines it admiringly.)

Now if there were a pair, I'd take them home to my wife. As it is . . .

(He throws the shoe away and trudges off right, pulling on the rope.)

Come on, Daisy!

Daisy is clearly some way behind, because she is still not in sight by the time HALLBJORN has disappeared offstage right. While all we can see is the rope stretched across the stage, tightening and slackening as the tired HALLBJORN pulls his reluctant animal to market, CARL leaps out from behind the boulder, retrieves the shoe and exits after the farmer. The lights fade just as Daisy is about to enter on the end of the rope . . .

Scene 5

A minute later: the same path, a hundred paces further on. CARL enters, right. Checks over his shoulder as before, deposits the shoe again and hides behind another convenient boulder. The farmer enters as before, pulling on the rope, and immediately spots the 'second' shoe.

HALLBJORN Well, I'll be . . . If it isn't the other half of the pair. *(He looks back over his shoulder wistfully.)* This is too good to miss. *(Idea!)*

I know what. I'll tie my ox to this boulder and nip back for the other shoe. My wife will be delighted!

(HALLBJORN loops the rope around CARL's boulder and exits left. CARL nips out, loosens the rope and exits after the farmer. Offstage there is the sound of bellowing, followed by the clatter of heavy oxen hooves receding into the distance.

HALLBJORN re-enters, holding only one shoe and scratching his head. It takes him only a second to realise what has happened.)

Oh, no! She'll kill me! *(He beats his head with his fist.)* Think, think, think! *(A second idea!)* Yes! I'll nip back to the farm, collect our other ox and take that to market instead. Daisy might be lost, but at least I can get a good price for Bluebell. Then, when I get back tomorrow, I'll blame her for letting Bluebell get stolen from under her nose while she slept . . .

Mulling over the finer points of his plan in his head, HALLBJORN turns back and sets off on his secret mission to collect the second ox as the lights fade . . .

ACTING: In groups of three, rehearse Scenes 4 and 5. First discuss how you will (a) employ the rope effectively, to suggest that there is indeed an ox on the end of it; (b) show Hallbjorn's changing reactions throughout the two scenes; and (c) manage Carl's nippy exits and entrances.

IMPROVISATION: In pairs, discuss another clever way in which Carl might steal one of Hallbjorn's oxen and act it out.

SCENE 6

The lights go up on the cabin interior and a burst of celebratory song from the gang – something like 'For he's a jolly good fellow!'.

CARL   Thank you, gentlemen. And, if I know Hallbjorn, I'm pretty confident that I can predict what he will do tomorrow . . .

They fill their cups and toast him again as the lights fade.

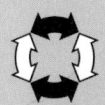

ACTING: In groups of six, freeze-frame the moment when the thieves are singing their song in celebration of Carl's success. Think carefully about each character's reactions and talk about what might be going through their heads at that moment. What is Carl thinking, for example? Or Thurid? How happy is Thorgaut? Then act out the scene. You could either use the song suggested in the stage directions, or find one of your own which has the same kind of message.

Scene 7

Dawn the following day. Lights up on the mountain path, as before, and HALLBJORN enters, pulling on his rope – as before. He stops to mop his brow and sits on a tree-stump.

HALLBJORN Just about here I found that confounded shoe and lost Daisy. *(Looking over his shoulder.)* I'll be damned if they catch me with that trick again. *(Producing a heavy hunting rifle from his pack, he shouts out, challengingly, to anyone within earshot.)* Just come and try, that's all!

(Suddenly, from somewhere behind him, there is the sound of a deep bellowing. He sits up and listens, hardly able to believe his ears. There is a second bellow.)

My lost ox! *(Leaping to his feet.)* Coming, Daisy, my love! Daddy's on his way!

(He hurriedly ties the rope round the tree-stump and runs off left, in the direction of the sound. CARL enters cautiously from right, unties the rope, picks up the discarded gun and exits. A second later we hear another bellow [realistic this time] and the sound of heavy ox hooves galloping off into the distance.)

(HALLBJORN re-enters, exhausted, perspiring and depressed.)

It must have been the wind. Never mind. Come on Bluebell . . . Bluebell? Oh no! I don't believe this. Bluebell! Bluebell!

And, as the lights dim, the poor farmer runs off in vain pursuit of his second lost ox.

Scene 8

The cabin interior, later that night. The THIEVES have plainly been celebrating again and are now relaxing, relishing their new recruit's success and dreamily contemplating a very rosy future indeed. CARL sits at the head of the table, enjoying their flattery.

SKAPTI	Two oxen in two days!	1
JOKULL	It's a miracle.	
CARL	Not at all, gentlemen. Simply a combination of good intelligence and animal cunning.	
THURID	*(In admiration.)* Ruthlessness and devil-may-care bravado.	
GRIM	Welcome to the Shadowdale Gang, Lad.	
SKAPTI	So what's our next job?	
	(An embarrassed silence falls. They all realise that THORGAUT has been standing aloof.)	
THORGAUT	Don't look at me. You have a new leader now: 'Lad Carl'. Ask him.	10
	(They look back at CARL. The lights dim as he begins his reign as the THIEVES' new leader.)	
CARL	Well, gentlemen, the way I see it is this . . .	
	Music.	

IMPROVISATION: In pairs, improvise the scene in which Hallbjorn returns to his wife having lost both oxen. How does she react? Does he tell the truth, or try to get himself out of trouble with a helpful lie?

SCENE 9

When the lights come up on the cabin, it is a scene of quiet industry – much poring over maps and stacking of ropes, weapons and baskets full of provisions.

CARL *(Calling them together.)* So. One final recap just to check everything's clear. Grim?

GRIM We assemble on the ridge above the village. Our signal to advance is the hooting of an owl and the cry of a wolf following the final chime of the church clock at midnight.

CARL Skapti?

SKAPTI The parish tax collections are in the strong-room in the assembly house. The only guard will be Agnar, an old caretaker, probably asleep.

CARL Jokull?

JOKULL We break in through the small window at the back, and overpower the old man.

CARL And Thorgaut?

(THORGAUT does not reply immediately. Either he is still resentful at having lost the leadership of the gang, or something is troubling him.)

Thorgaut?

THORGAUT You and I break the lock of the front door from the inside . . .

GRIM And we drag the coffers out on to the sledge – and away.

CARL Excellent. Any questions?

THORGAUT	Just one. You haven't said what we do with Agnar, the old caretaker.
SKAPTI	Kill him. Something quiet.
JOKULL	Tie him up and dump him out the back – let him freeze to death.
GRIM	Whatever happens, we can't afford to leave him there to identify us.
	(They all look at THORGAUT.)
CARL	Thorgaut?
THORGAUT	*(He has made an important decision.)* No. He's an old man. It's not right.
GRIM	That doesn't usually bother you.
THORGAUT	It bothers me today: I say no violence.
	(They are interrupted as the clock begins to chime.)
CARL	Eleven o'clock. Load the sledge, then let's be about it.
	They collect their equipment and all leave the cabin except for CARL, who goes upstairs. In the silence of the now empty room we hear, from somewhere above, the flapping of a bird's wings. As CARL comes back down the stairs, THORGAUT returns for his gun and the two men find themselves facing each other. CARL smiles, slaps THORGAUT on the shoulder and exits. THORGAUT, still troubled, collects his gun and follows, as the lights dim to blackout.

Scene 10

In almost complete blackness we can just make out that we are in a large timbered hall. A village clock chimes twelve. We hear the hooting of an owl and the howling of a wolf; then, a few seconds later, the sound of wood being splintered. A rectangular patch of starry sky appears in the back wall and a shadowy figure climbs through the window. He helps in three others and they stand, waiting for orders. When they speak, it is in tense whispers.

GRIM	Which way's the strong-room, Carl?	1
SKAPTI	He said straight in front.	
JOKULL	As far as I can make out, that's just a blank wall.	

THORGAUT   This doesn't feel right . . . Carl? . . . Lad?

(There is a deafening and blinding burst of gunfire, then silence.)

(CARL enters, carrying a lantern, which illuminates the scene. GRIM, SKAPTI and JOKULL lie dead in a pool of blood; THORGAUT is slumped against the back wall, not wounded, but totally stunned and incapable of movement. Appearing from behind the heavy assembly house furniture are six VILLAGERS, carrying still smoking guns.)

(HALLBJORN enters and hands CARL a slatted box. CARL lifts it to his face and we can just hear a gentle cooing and the fluttering of wings.)

(THORGAUT staggers forward and stares long and hard into CARL's face.)

THORGAUT   You betrayed us . . . We trusted you.

CARL says nothing, but takes some seed from his pocket and feeds the pigeon. As the lights dim to blackness, we hear the peaceful sound of the bird as it settles down for the night inside its wooden cage.

ARTWORK: Imagine you were making a film of this play. Draw four or five frames of a storyboard to represent the events of Scene 10. The first frame might look like the picture on page 22.

DISCUSSION: What exactly has happened? Discuss the following questions in pairs:
(a) What must have taken place after Carl's successful theft of the oxen?
(b) As they are getting ready to leave for the raid, Thorgaut is troubled about something: what do you think it is? Is he beginning to see through Carl? Is he worried that the raid might fail under their new leader? Is he sulking because he has lost the leadership? Does he have misgivings about how they should deal with the old caretaker?
(c) How do the villagers know to expect the thieves and lie in wait for them?

WRITING: Write the report which might appear in the following day's newspaper (decide first whether it is a broadsheet or a tabloid). Include a full account of the events as Carl might relate them himself and include quotes from other characters such as Hallbjorn.

DISCUSSION:
1   *Carl's methods:* What are your opinions about Carl's methods for catching the thieves? Hold a class discussion in which you consider the following questions, among others:
    • Someone who infiltrates a group of criminals and deliberately gets them involved in a crime so that they can be arrested is known by a French term: *agent provocateur*. Do you feel that this method for catching law-breakers is unfair, or does 'the end justify the means'?
    • Thorgaut is shocked that Carl has betrayed them and sees him as a traitor; how do you feel about Carl's actions?
2   *Crime and punishment:* Is it appropriate that Thorgaut should survive while the others in the gang are all killed? Why might the writer have chosen to end the play in that way?

Dramascripts

The Testing of Tseng

Dramatised by
JOHN O'CONNOR

Where the Tale Comes From

Set in the far-off days of imperial China, *The Testing of Tseng* tells the story of an arrogant and conceited young man who is given the opportunity to fulfil his ambitions and then learn from his mistakes.

Based upon an ancient Chinese tale, the play suggests that we might be able to avoid being locked into an endless cycle of wrongdoing. But it also asks us to consider whether it is solely the threat of punishment – in this world or the next – which can keep people on the straight and narrow . . .

The Characters

(in order of appearance)

OLD MAN*

TSENG CHUNG KI *a clerk in the Office of Public Health and Sanitation.*

EMPEROR'S BODYGUARD

LING, YAMMO *servants working in the imperial palace.*

CHANG FEY *a minister.*

TA SI, YUEN, PAN KU, FU SI *other ministers and courtiers.*

PING-WUR *Yuen's wife.*

BEGGAR (*also* **EMPEROR)**

1ST ROBBER

2ND ROBBER

3RD ROBBER

4TH ROBBER

EMPEROR OF THE DEAD

SCROLL-READER

YOUNG MAN

OTHER COURTIERS AND SERVANTS IN THE IMPERIAL PALACE*

* indicates non-speaking part

The Testing of Tseng

Scene 1

The scene is a bare hut made of rushes. A pot simmers over a small fire, but the place is otherwise empty except for a low bed and a mat in the centre of the floor. The room's only occupant is an OLD MAN. He sits cross-legged on the mat and is quite motionless, staring fixedly ahead of him and showing on his face not the faintest trace of emotion. The only sound is the low bubbling of the pot, which contains a thin soup.

Suddenly two things happen. There is a clap of thunder. And the OLD MAN slowly smiles. Then we hear the first pitter-patter of rain falling on the rush roof, and within a few seconds the rain outside is coming down in torrents.

Still the OLD MAN sits motionless, like one of the golden lions that guard the imperial palace gates. But his solitude is about to be broken.

A young man shoves open the door and stands just inside the hut, looking outwards to the falling rain, trying to shake himself dry while cursing his misfortune and the country's weather. He is quite well dressed, according to the fashion of the land in those days, wearing a silk tunic and smart coat, and has only entered the hut in order to shelter from the rain-storm.

SCENE 1

| TSENG | *(Muttering to himself.)* Another minute out there and my clothes would be ruined. Can't they do anything about the roads around here? The mud's appalling. New shoes! Look at them! | 1 |

(As he removes his coat and turns to find somewhere to hang it up, he notices for the first time that the hovel is occupied.)

Oh. Didn't see you there. Don't mind if I shelter for a minute or two, I suppose? Caught in the storm – wet through. The name's Tseng. I'm . . . in government, you know. Civil service. My father's in the Treasury. *(He looks out of the door again.)* What's the name of this hole, anyway?

(Still the OLD MAN does not respond, but stares out fixedly as before.)

I said, what's . . .

(TSENG stops, turns and looks at the OLD MAN. Then he walks over and bends down to inspect him. He slowly waves his hand in front of the OLD MAN's face, strolls around him to complete his inspection from all angles and then looks at him for a second or two from a distance.)

Hmm. Either deaf and blind, or merely stupid. *(He laughs.)* Possibly all three! *(Looking around.)* What a place! How do people live like this? And I'm stuck here until this storm gives over because I haven't got a carriage . . . Yes, that's what I want. Proper respect. A position that befits my talents and breeding. *(He goes to the door again and looks out wistfully.)* A high-powered official in the Emperor's court, not a

 **the Treasury** *The government department which looks after finance.*

THE TESTING OF TSENG   SCENE 1

second-grade clerk, a dead-end pen-pusher! One day ... One day there'll be a sound of hooves outside and a knock on the door. It'll be the Emperor's Private Secretary with an invitation ... an offer of a post in government ... And that means wealth and power. Then I can do exactly what I want ...

(TSENG leaves the door and goes over to the fire. He stirs the pot miserably and looks at the OLD MAN.)

Any of this to spare, old man? You see, I missed my lunch. We always dine at twelve – in the special Civil Service canteen, naturally – and, what with this foul weather ... Of course, this is hardly what I'm used to, but, as you'll appreciate, I don't have much choice ...

(Again there is no response from the OLD MAN. TSENG shrugs his shoulders and begins to ladle some of the soup into a wooden bowl.)

Ah, well, since you don't seem to want it yourself, it'll save it going to waste.

(TSENG sits on the bed. As he takes his first mouthful of the soup, there is another almighty crash of thunder. But TSENG is hungry and takes no notice.)

Not bad, actually. Rice, is it? And what are these grassy bits floating around? *(He takes another mouthful.)* I think I can honestly say, old man ... *(Another mouthful.)* that I've never tasted such *(He searches for the right word.)* ... **unusual** soup in my entire life ... But it serves its purpose, no doubt.

(As he drains the last of his bowlful, the beating of the rain fades away and there is a moment's silence. Then, faintly at first, but getting louder, is the unmistakable sound of approaching horses ... and the wheels of a carriage ...)

31

SCENE 1

Horses? Here?

(The carriage is heard to stop outside. There is a sound of footsteps and then three heavy blows on the door. TSENG is frightened and looks to the OLD MAN for support.)

I . . . I think you've got visitors. They can't be for me – no-one knows I'm here. *(The visitors knock again.)* Unless . . . *(A look of fear creeps across TSENG's face.)* Oh, no. They've found out about the pens. I only took three from the office and I meant to give them back . . . *(Three more knocks.)* It wasn't really stealing! Old man! Old man! Help me!

(But the door begins to creak open and TSENG stands rooted to the spot in terror, for the figure who enters is none other than one of the EMPEROR's personal bodyguard, armoured from head to foot in leather and shining steel. When TSENG finds his voice, it is almost inaudible.)

I borrowed them, you see . . . The nibs were almost blunt and I didn't think they'd be any use . . . I could pay you back. Yes! Why don't I take a cut in salary? Or even have no salary at all for a month or so . . . Or a year . . . Or . . .

BODYGUARD *(In a deep and booming voice.)* Do I address Tseng Chung Ki, clerk of the second grade in the Office of Public Health and Sanitation?

TSENG *(Timidly.)* Yes.

BODYGUARD *(Producing a scroll.)* By the powers invested in me as Personal Bodyguard to His Most Impressive Majesty

 **Public Health and Sanitation** *Tseng's department is in charge of the drains.*

THE TESTING OF TSENG SCENE 1

	The Emperor Hi-Lung-Yo, I require you to give attention to the contents of this Imperial Scroll, being a communication from the Secretariat of Employment, Promotions and Ignominious Dismissals.
TSENG	Dismissals! I've been sacked! I wish I'd never seen those pens! I . . .
BODYGUARD	*(He reads.)* This is to request and command Tseng Chung Ki, clerk of the second grade in the Office of Public Health and Sanitation, to report without delay to the Imperial Palace, where, in view of his excellent and most noticeable service, the said Tseng Chung Ki will be promoted to the rank of Chief Minister in the Office of Finance and Public Affairs. *(As TSENG stands open-mouthed, the BODYGUARD bows almost to the floor.)* Chief Minister in Waiting Tseng! A carriage is ready when it will suit you to depart. *(He bows again and exits.)*
	(For a few moments TSENG can do no more than open and close his mouth like one of the golden carp in the imperial fishpond. Then he walks in a daze towards the door. He is about to leave, but suddenly and unexpectedly rounds on the OLD MAN, who has been sitting silently throughout.)
TSENG	You see, old man! What did I tell you! I knew I wouldn't be a stinking little clerk for long. Wait till I get back! I'll show that supervising clerk a thing or two! Thinks he can bully me, does he? Making me copy out a whole letter again just because I spilt a bit

90

100

110

Secretariat *Government department or office.*

Ignominious *Humiliating, shameful.*

of ink on the corner! He'll have other things to think about when he's languishing in the imperial dungeons! *(He snatches his coat from the wall, strides to the door and then pauses and turns to the OLD MAN.)* And as for you – you and your gruesome soup! Think yourself lucky I'm not having you flogged for your dumb insolence!

He exits, slamming the door behind him. The OLD MAN smiles.

120

languishing *Suffering and fading away.*

dumb insolence *A crime in the armed forces: someone can be punished for saying nothing but appearing to be offensive and insulting.*

ARTWORK: Imagine you were making a film of this play. Storyboard the opening stage directions in four key frames (perhaps including at least one exterior shot, showing the hut and the dreadful weather).

DISCUSSION AND WRITING: From the things that Tseng says to the old man, what have you learned about (a) his real job; (b) his ambitions; and (c) the petty crimes that he has committed at work?

Draft the end-of-year report that Tseng's boss might write, in which he comments on how well Tseng does his job and his attitudes in the workplace.

ACTING: In groups of three, act out the scene from the moment Tseng hears horses approaching ('Horses? Here?' – line 62) to the end. First decide what different reactions Tseng should have at various moments (a) before the Bodyguard enters; (b) during the announcement; and (c) after the Bodyguard has left. Think also about the old man's reactions.

WRITING: Draw up a time-line which represents the main events of the story. Include what has happened to Tseng in Scene 1 (call this Year 1, Day 1) and add the events of each scene as you read it. It will help to discuss with a partner how much time you think might have passed between scenes.

SCENE 2

A wing of the imperial palace. To the left are tall, slender windows through which can be seen the turrets of the city; to the right a massive and intricately carved wooden door. In the centre, an impressive golden throne, raised up on a carpeted platform. Servants are scurrying around, obviously preparing the room for some important event. Two servants – LING and YAMMO – seem more relaxed than the others and chat as they work, pausing occasionally to lean on their brooms.

LING I could cope if it was every month. Once a fortnight, even. But every other day . . . ! 1

YAMMO Yes, he certainly likes his banquets, does High Chamberlain Tseng.

LING I mean, take the last one – what was he called? – Ling-pei. One banquet a month and extras for eclipses. Nothing wrong with that. Perfectly acceptable.

YAMMO You can forgive extras for eclipses.

LING	Extras for eclipses I can tolerate. But this! This is wanton excess!	10
YAMMO	Wanton excess, as you say.	
LING	How long's he been here? A year? Eighteen months?	
YAMMO	Must be. At least eighteen months.	
LING	And would you say he was popular?	
YAMMO	*(Thinks carefully for a moment.)* No. Not popular, no.	
LING	And why not?	
YAMMO	Does it have something to do with his wanton excess?	
LING	It does have something to do with that, yes. It is also not unrelated to his freedom with the executioner's axe.	20
YAMMO	Ah, the axe.	
LING	I've lost count of the men he's had beheaded.	
YAMMO	Thirty-seven.	
LING	What?	
YAMMO	Thirty-seven.	
	(Pause. LING looks at YAMMO.)	
LING	How did you know that?	
YAMMO	It's in the paper, look. *(Produces a newspaper and reads.)* 'Thirty-seventh traitor to be beheaded at dawn today. Banquet six-thirty. Rain expected in Dang-jin Province.'	30

wanton excess *Overdoing things irresponsibly.*

THE TESTING OF TSENG SCENE 2

LING Let me see that. *(He takes the paper off him and reads.)* 'The most notorious traitor Hur San is to be beheaded at dawn this morning by order of the great and mighty High Chamberlain Tseng Chung Ki . . .' *(Looks up.)* What'd he done?

YAMMO Who knows? They never say.

LING *(Carries on reading.)* 'The execution will be followed by a banquet . . .'

(LING sighs and looks at YAMMO, who shrugs his shoulders.)

'. . . followed by a banquet and the disposing of honours. Traitor Hur San is the thirty-seventh to be executed since High Chamberlain Tseng Chung Ki came to office.' *(Trying to recall something.)* Hur San . . . Wasn't he one of Tseng's oldest friends?

YAMMO *(Nods.)* At school together. Seems that Hur San kept reminding Tseng of his humble origins.

LING So he had his head chopped off?

YAMMO Tseng has declared it treason to remind him that he was once a talentless second grade clerk with an unpleasant habit of filching everybody else's pens.

LING I take it he didn't phrase it exactly like that.

YAMMO Not exactly like that, no. The Decree was something to do with Bringing the Office of High Chamberlain into Disrepute.

 **humble origins** *Tseng had come from an ordinary family, not part of the aristocracy.*

filching *Stealing.*

LING	If anybody's done that, it's Tseng. He's raised taxes twenty-two times, banished half the people who oppose him and executed the rest! That is what I would call an abuse of power!	60
	(Trumpets suddenly herald the entrance of TSENG and about a dozen courtiers through the carved doors. He is magnificently dressed in embroidered silks that shimmer as he walks. At the first note of the trumpets, LING and YAMMO throw their brooms behind the throne and prostrate themselves. TSENG walks over them and takes his place on the throne.)	
TSENG	Where is Minister Chang Fey?	70
	(A very smarmy courtier comes forward.)	
CHANG	Here, High Chamberlain Tseng.	
TSENG	You have a request for us, have you not?	
CHANG	A humble one, your excellency.	
TSENG	Say on. You cannot speak of reason to Tseng Chung Ki and be ignored. What would you have?	
CHANG	Since the – er, sudden 'retirement' of Hur San this morning . . .	
TSENG	Yes?	
CHANG	. . . Well, the post of Collector of Taxes for So-jen Province has become vacant . . . And I wondered, most excellent Tseng . . .	80
TSENG	*(Interrupting him.)* Minister Chang.	

banished Forced to leave the country and spend the rest of their lives abroad.

prostrate themselves Throw themselves to the floor and lie face-down in submission.

THE TESTING OF TSENG — SCENE 2

CHANG   Yes, excellency?

TSENG   The post of Collector of Taxes is a demanding one.

CHANG   Oh, I am aware of that, excellency, I . . .

TSENG   It requires some particularly difficult arithmetical calculations . . . How much to take in taxes from the rich, how much to pay oneself as an annual salary . . . and, of course . . .   90

CHANG   *(He understands perfectly.)* How much to donate to the coffers of the Office of High Chamberlain, excellency?

TSENG   Precisely.

CHANG   *(He thinks carefully before replying.)* I hear that there has been an exceptionally fruitful harvest in So-jen Province this year, excellency. It would be only right and proper that the most essential and exalted Office of the High Chamberlain should benefit.

TSENG   What a very good idea, Collector of Taxes Chang.

(CHANG and TSENG smile at each other as CHANG backs away from the throne, bowing as he does so. Some of the other courtiers secretly exchange very unhappy and despairing looks.)   100

(Next, a very timid courtier approaches the throne and bows. TSENG is clearly not pleased to see him.)

Well?

TA SI   *(Clearly frightened.)* Councillor Ta Si, your excellency.

TSENG   *(Impatiently.)* Yes?

 **exalted** *Eminent, superior.*

TA SI	*(Hesitantly.)* It's . . . It's about my country house, excellency . . .	
	(TSENG's expression changes to one of barely controlled fury.)	
TSENG	**Your** country house?	
TA SI	Well . . . The one I lent you during the visit of the Emperor of Tibet . . .	
	(TSENG doesn't reply.)	
	The House of the White Gables, excellency . . . The one you admired so much . . .	
TSENG	What about it?	
TA SI	May I have it back, excellency? . . . That is, if your excellency has finished with it. It has been in my family for many generations and my mother . . .	
TSENG	**Your** house, councillor? The one you donated to the Office of the High Chamberlain for use on state occasions?	
TA SI	Donated?	
TSENG	Saying that you would rather your head were struck from your shoulders than that the house should be kept back from public use.	
	(TA SI stands silently for a moment. Then his head drops and in a barely audible whisper he replies.)	
TA SI	My family will be honoured if the House of the White Gables were to remain under the care of the Office of the High Chamberlain.	
TSENG	Splendid. In that case, I think I'll take a few friends up there this week-end. Oh, don't bother to remove the furnishings, Ta Si. We'll need something to sleep on!	

THE TESTING OF TSENG   **SCENE 2**

	(TSENG laughs at his joke and, after a split-second's pause, the courtiers – with the exception of TA SI – join in. TSENG carries on laughing as he sweeps from the room [closely followed by CHANG FEY and treading, en route, on the still prostrate LING and YAMMO]. As the great doors close behind them, the courtiers' laughter stops abruptly and, in its place, we hear a soft weeping sound. It is TA SI, bewailing the loss of his family home. One by one, the courtiers approach him.) 140
YUEN	Sorry, old chap, but what could we do?
PAN KU	You're hardly the first, but I suppose that's no consolation to you. 150
FU SI	He stole my new junk last month. Said it was required for naval defensive purposes, and the next I knew, he was entertaining his friends on a fishing trip.
YUEN	There really isn't anything we can do.
	(A powerful-looking woman standing at the back can take it no longer. Like a grumbling volcano, she suddenly erupts.)
PING-WUR	You pusillanimous poltroons!
YUEN	Wife!
PING-WUR	You craven cowards! 160
YUEN	Ping-wur, remember your place!
PING-WUR	You lily-livered . . . What begins with L?

en route On his way through.

junk *A flat-bottomed sailing ship.*

pusillanimous poltroons! *Timid and spiritless cowards.*

craven *Another word for cowardly (like 'pusillanimous' and 'lily-livered' below).*

YAMMO	*(Still face-down on the floor.)* Lunatics?
PING-WUR	No . . .
YAMMO	Lounge-lizards?
PING-WUR	Not exactly . . .
YUEN	Who is that man?
YAMMO	Limp-wrists?
PING-WUR	Excellent! You lily-livered limp-wrists!
YUEN	I say, steady on!
PING-WUR	In the name of the gods, do something! Don't stand around yammering, like a bunch of bewildered . . .
YAMMO	Bed-bugs?
PING-WUR	Get up a petition! Form a union! Demand to see the Emperor!
YUEN	But, wife, the Emperor appointed this man.
FU SI	If we complain about him, it will look as though we are criticising his choice.
PAN KU	That would never do.
	(She looks at them in turn.)
PING-WUR	Words fail me. *(She turns to go.)*
YAMMO	You could try calling them . . .
THE THREE MEN	Be quiet!
	(PING-WUR exits, followed by the three agitated men and the still sobbing TA SI. LING and YAMMO remain on the floor for a moment. Then . . .)

170

180

 **petition** *A formal written request, signed by large numbers of people.*

THE TESTING OF TSENG SCENE 2

LING Have they gone?

YAMMO I think so.

(They get up.)

LING What was all that 'limp-wrists' and 'bed-bugs' business about?

YAMMO I thought she needed a bit of help, that's all.

LING *(Retrieving their brooms from behind the throne.)* You'll get yourself into serious trouble one of these days – you know that, don't you? Come on. Let's go home. I've had enough excitement to last me the week. *(As they leave.)* Have you ever thought about chucking all this in and becoming a travelling orange-seller? I think I'm beginning to find this profession a bit stressful.

YAMMO Oh, I don't know. You get to lie down a lot.

(Once again we hear the imperial trumpets, heralding the re-entrance of TSENG and the courtiers.)

LING Talking of which . . .

(LING and YAMMO prostrate themselves again and TSENG enters – and walks over them again – on his way to the throne.)

TSENG Sorry to call you back so quickly, gentleman, but it occurred to me just now, as I was feeding little bits of my former friend Hur San to the imperial carp, that my two years as High Chamberlain would shortly be coming to an end.

(The courtiers can hardly disguise their delight and relief.)

PAN KU We were aware of that, excellency.

YUEN It will indeed be a tragedy.

FU SI A great loss to the province.

SCENE 2

ALL TOGETHER But . . . *(They shrug their shoulders, as if to say 'We're terribly disappointed, but those are the rules: what can we do about it?')*

TSENG 'But . . .'? What do you mean, 'But . . .'? 220

(Silence. The men look at each other fearfully, wondering what he has got up his sleeve this time.)

But what?

YAMMO *(Muffled, still face down on the floor.)* But there you go . . . ? But all good things come to an end . . . ? But that's the way the cookie . . .

TSENG *(Screams.)* **Who is that man?**

YUEN A servant, excellency. Shall I have him removed?

TSENG Removed? **Removed?** It's his head that will be removed! 230

(But suddenly TSENG controls his temper, breathes deeply and smiles . . .)

But, as I am in an exceptionally good humour, I shall demonstrate the mercy for which I am justly famous and commute his sentence to banishment for life.

(YAMMO whimpers.)

You . . . Whatever your name is. Stand up.

(YAMMO does so.)

You are banished, in accordance with the most exalted wishes of the High Chamberlain *(TSENG leans over in YAMMO's direction and smiles at him horribly.)* – 240

 **commute** *Reduce his sentence to something less severe.*

	i.e. me – to the outer wastes of . . . of . . . Well, of whatever lies outside the civilised reaches of Dang-jin Province.	
YAMMO	*(Still whimpering.)* Thank you, excellency.	
	(YAMMO walks disconsolately towards the door.)	
TSENG	*(Noticing LING, still prostrate on the floor.)* And take your dirty washing with you!	
	(YAMMO returns, picks up LING by the scruff of the neck, and they both back out through the exit, bowing as they do so.)	250
	Where were we? Ah, yes. You were expressing your inexpressible disappointment that, in accordance with tradition, I, Tseng Chung Ki, of honourable family and extremely impressive education, should be bludgeoned into resigning as High Chamberlain when my term of office ends next month.	
	(They look at each other suspiciously.)	
PAN KU	Were we, excellency?	
TSENG	*(A harder edge coming into his voice.)* Well, **I think** you were, Pan Ku . . . And, unless I am very mistaken, I think you were about to suggest that two years is far too short a time in which to benefit from my wisdom, mercy and all-round jolly sound management?	260
	(They look at each other miserably. It is only too clear what is required of them. YUEN steps forward.)	
YUEN	*(Muttering unhappily.)* Excellency . . . May I, on behalf of the grateful people of Dang-jin Province, request	

i.e. *In other words.*

bludgeoned *Forced (like being hit with something heavy).*

	that you extend your rule as High Chamberlain for a further ... *(He looks up to TSENG for guidance.)* Two ...? *(TSENG frowns.)* Five ...? *(The frown does not disappear. YUAN swallows hard.)* May I suggest that you take on the exalted post of High Chamberlain ... *(He struggles to utter the final words.)* ... for ever?
TSENG	*(As though having to make a difficult decision.)* For ever ...? Goodness me, that is a tough one ... But, since you would clearly be desolate with disappointment were I to refuse your freely made request, I shall – reluctantly – take the burden upon my shoulders. *(He rubs his hands together and then says, in a cheerful and brisk manner.)* Well, that's that then. Anyone for a banquet?
	(He rises, but, at that moment the doors open and YUEN's wife, PING-WUR, enters, accompanied by an old BEGGAR. The councillors gasp in horror and all heads turn to TSENG to observe his reaction. At first speechless with anger, TSENG points at the BEGGAR, his hand trembling. When he finds his voice it is a barely audible whisper.)
	What on earth is that?
PING-WUR	A beggar, excellency. I found him at the door.
TSENG	But what's he doing in my palace?
PING-WUR	I have invited him to the banquet, excellency.
TSENG	*(Almost speechless.)* To the ...?
PING-WUR	The banquet. You will recall the ancient laws of hospitality. Any beggar who seeks alms from the Office of the High Chamberlain ...

desolate Extremely miserable.

alms Money or food given to the poor out of charity.

THE TESTING OF TSENG SCENE 2

TSENG	*(Impatiently and angrily.)* Yes, yes. I know, I know. But you don't honestly expect me to take them seriously, do you? Invite that bundle of rags and **vermin** to a banquet given in **my** honour? 300
PING-WUR	It is a tradition of our forefathers, excellency. I ask you for the second time . . .
TSENG	I don't give a fig for our forefathers. And, unless you want to become a foremother at dawn tomorrow, I suggest . . .
PING-WUR	For the third time, I ask you to observe the ancient laws.
TSENG	And for the third time I say no!

 **vermin** *Fleas and parasites.*

SCENE 2

(There is a terrific clap of thunder. Everyone except PING-WUR and the BEGGAR fall to their knees. Slowly the BEGGAR removes his ragged cloak and lets it drop to the ground to reveal a dignified old man with a white beard that reaches to his waist. It is the EMPEROR.)

TSENG *(Whispering, terrified.)* Your imperial highness . . .

EMPEROR Too long have we hidden ourselves away in our palace, too long pored over books and kept ourselves with our own thoughts. We had heard, but did not believe. Did not choose to be concerned, rather. Poor people. How you have suffered. And you. *(Turning to TSENG.)* You have abused the power entrusted to you. For which our sentence is that you be banished from the company of men with no hope of return. *(TSENG grovels at the EMPEROR's feet, pleading for mercy, but the EMPEROR is immovable.)* If you are ever found in our empire again, you will suffer the same fate as those poor men and women whose lives you have so cruelly taken. Be thankful for the Emperor's mercy, and in the long nights ahead of you, think on your misdeeds and learn to be better.

As the EMPEROR utters his final words, there is a great howling of wind and the scene dims to darkness.

LANGUAGE: Ping-wur's insulting expressions for the cowardly courtiers are striking because of her careful choice of words. Find all her different synonyms for 'cowardly'. Can you think of others she might have used?
She also employs alliteration to great effect – though Yammo has to help her out. Make up some other alliterative expressions to insult people, similar to 'pusillanimous poltroons' and 'lily-livered limp-wrists'. (These are to do with cowardice: you could invent others to do with different vices, such as meanness, boastfulness or laziness.)

FREEZE-FRAME: The moment when 'the beggar' enters can be highly dramatic: Tseng is furious and disgusted; the courtiers are terrified how he might react; Ping-wur is pleased with the effect she has created. Freeze-frame the scene in groups of ten, bringing out all the individual reactions.

Scene 3

When some light returns, we are on a desert road. TSENG, now wearing a very ragged and mud-spattered version of his silken costume, trudges wearily into sight. Throwing down his heavy pack, he collapses exhausted by the wayside.

TSENG	Undone! Ruined by that meddling woman! Well, I'm not finished yet.	1
1ST ROBBER	*(Offstage.)* Oh yes, you are!	
	(There is a burst of rough laughter and a band of ROBBERS enter from all sides. TSENG leaps to his feet but is surrounded.)	
TSENG	What do you want?	
1ST ROBBER	The usual: hand over your purse.	
TSENG	*(Handing it over.)* You're welcome to it. I spent the last yuan three days ago.	10
	(He gives it to the 1st ROBBER, who shakes it, turns it inside out and disappointedly throws it to his friend.)	
1ST ROBBER	He's right.	
2ND ROBBER	What about the bag?	
TSENG	You won't find much in there, either. A spare cloak, rather more threadbare than the one I've got on, and the remains of today's breakfast. The bread was so hard I couldn't eat it.	
4TH ROBBER	What are these? *(He has taken out some pens.)*	

yuan *The currency in China.*

SCENE 3

TSENG	A special parting gift. They thought it was funny.
3RD ROBBER	This is hopeless.
1ST ROBBER	Come on, there's a coach coming through the valley tonight. This one's a waste of time.
	(The ROBBERS put their knives and cudgels away and prepare to leave. But TSENG, having escaped robbery and death, has come to see them as his only means of survival.)
TSENG	Wait! Take me with you! Let me join the gang!
2ND ROBBER	You?
	(They laugh at him.)
	You haven't even got the sense to steal a decent breakfast! What good would you be to us?
TSENG	You'd be surprised. I'm not afraid to kill a man. *(The ROBBERS stop in their tracks . . . And then slowly turn to stare at him as he speaks.)* I've done in thirty-seven in the past couple of years, and banished a whole lot more.
	(There is a silence as they take in what he has just revealed. Then . . .)
3RD ROBBER	What's your name?
TSENG	Never mind my name. Can I . . .
4TH ROBBER	It can't be.
	(They have now returned to circle TSENG and for the first time look carefully at his face.)
1ST ROBBER	I don't believe it.
2ND ROBBER	Delivered like this into our hands.
TSENG	What do you mean? Believe what? Delivered who?

THE TESTING OF TSENG SCENE 3

1ST ROBBER   If we are not mistaken – and we are not – we have the honour to entertain Tseng Chung Ki . . .

2ND ROBBER   . . . his excellency the Lord High Chamberlain . . .

3RD ROBBER   . . . of the province of Dang-jin.

TSENG   How do you know who I am? Anyway, what of it? Are you going to help me or not?

4TH ROBBER   Like you helped us, you mean?

TSENG   I don't know what you're talking about. I've never met you before.

4TH ROBBER   Oh yes, you have. But I don't blame you for not recognising us. A year in this wilderness changes a man, and not altogether for the better. Look at us carefully, High Chamberlain Tseng, and try ever so hard.

(TSENG looks at each one in turn. As he moves from face to face, the terrifying truth begins to dawn upon him . . .)

TSENG   *(To 1st ROBBER.)* You were . . .

1ST ROBBER   Yes, excellency. You banished me because you wanted my house.

TSENG   *(To 2nd ROBBER.)* And you . . .

2ND ROBBER   You banished me for disagreeing with you.

TSENG   *(To 3rd ROBBER.)* I remember you . . .

3RD ROBBER   You banished me for talking about your humble childhood.

TSENG   *(To 4th ROBBER.)* But you. I can't quite recall . . .

4TH ROBBER   I was the first. You banished me because, as Chief Clerk in the Office of Public Health and Sanitation . . .

TSENG   *(The awful truth dawns.)* Oh, no . . .

4TH ROBBER	. . . I had caught you stealing . . . *(He holds one up in front of TSENG's face . . .)* pens.
	(TSENG looks at them all again, horrified.)
TSENG	What are you going to do? I showed mercy to you. At least I didn't have you executed.
1ST ROBBER	Mercy? You call this mercy?
2ND ROBBER	Banishing your friends to a wilderness and turning honest men into robbers?
3RD ROBBER	Death is merciful compared to this, Tseng.
4TH ROBBER	And we will be merciful. We will show you the mercy that you denied us.
TSENG	Death.
1ST ROBBER	Death. *(They each take out a knife.)* Quick and . . . *(They crowd round and plunge their knives into him.)* . . . merciful.

The ROBBERS stand silently looking at his body for a moment and then leave. There is a slow blackout.

Scene 4

A flickering reddish glow spreads slowly across the stage and we begin to hear the sound of a constantly burning fire. TSENG groans, rubs his body and then sits up, startled.

TSENG I'm not dead! **I'm not dead!**

(He jumps to his feet, laughing, but his celebration is cut short as he stumbles into an obstacle that he had not noticed before. It is a black throne and on it sits a daunting figure in black robes and a silver crown. Beside it stands another figure in grey, holding a great scroll.)

Who . . . Who are you?

EMPEROR OF THE DEAD I think you know who I am, Tseng Chung Ki.

TSENG You . . . You are the Emperor of the Dead . . . So they did kill me after all . . .

(TSENG backs away from the throne and looks around, perhaps hoping for some way out, but knowing in his heart that there is none.)

What happens to me now?

(The EMPEROR OF THE DEAD does not reply immediately, but receives a scroll from the silent figure standing next to him. He looks at TSENG for a moment before speaking.)

EMPEROR OF THE DEAD This is the register of the deeds of mankind. What will it say, do you think, about Tseng Chung Ki?

(TSENG's mouth opens, but he cannot speak. The EMPEROR OF THE DEAD hands the scroll back to the figure in grey, who opens it and reads. His voice is terrifyingly without emotion.)

SCROLL-READER   Crime the first. You betrayed your friends and sent many to their deaths.

EMPEROR OF THE DEAD   Your punishment, Tseng Chung Ki, is that devils shall come for you and take you to a place where you will be thrown into a cauldron of boiling oil. As you writhe in the seething liquid, your tender flesh will suffer the most unbearable agonies and you will certainly scream for a termination of your torments. But, being already dead, the wished-for end will be excrutiatingly delayed.

(TSENG falls to the ground, weeping in terror.)

His second crime?

SCROLL-READER   Crime the second. You sent many honest men into banishment, where they were forced to live by violence and theft.

EMPEROR OF THE DEAD   Your punishment will be to climb the hill of knives. As you toil to the top, goaded by devils, the soles of your feet will be torn to shreds by the points that you walk upon, while more devils in the likeness of those you banished will stab you and jeer at your misery. His third crime?

SCROLL-READER   Crime the third. You stole, during your time of office, a million gold pieces.

EMPEROR OF THE DEAD   Your punishment will be to watch every last gold piece that you stole, melted down, and then to suffer the agony of having it poured, cup after cup, down your choking throat.

   **excrutiatingly** *Extremely painfully.*

THE TESTING OF TSENG SCENE 4

TSENG (Crawling towards the throne.) Oh, forgive me! I wasn't really a bad man. I was weak. You must understand that. I had never had power before, working as a snivelling little copy-clerk, having to bow and scrape before the meanest civil servant. It all went to my head. I've learned my lesson now. Oh, give me one more chance, I beg you!

EMPEROR OF THE DEAD You have had your chances, Tseng Chung Ki. *(He stands and nods to the figure in grey, who bows and exits.)* I shall leave you to ponder on your crimes. But you do not have long. Even as I speak, the cauldron begins to boil . . .

He leaves and we too can now hear the ominous sound of bubbling liquid. As it grows louder, TSENG's cries of terror increase, until, with the bubbling at its loudest and a mighty scream from TSENG, the stage is plunged into blackness.

ACTING: In groups of five, act out the sequence in which the robbers recognise Tseng and kill him (from the moment when they laugh at him on page 50). Decide first how the robbers will behave as they begin to realise who the stranger is (look carefully at the stage directions) and then work out how to stage the killing both effectively and practically.

ACTING: What voices should the Emperor of the Dead and his Scroll-reader have? Something like Darth Vadar, for example? Experiment with different voices and then perform the scene.

ARTWORK: What should the Emperor of the Dead and the Scroll-reader look like? Draw sketches to show your ideas for possible costumes and decide what to do about their faces. Should they wear masks, for example, or might it be more effective to use make-up, so that we can see their expressions?

ARTWORK: In films we are sometimes allowed to 'see' what is in a character's mind. Draw four or five frames of a storyboard to show the torments that Tseng might be imagining as the Emperor of the Dead describes them (lines 26–50).

DISCUSSION AND IMPROVISATION: Are the torments imposed by the Emperor of the Dead fair punishments, bearing in mind Tseng's crimes? In groups of eight, stage a few moments of a trial in which Tseng or his defence counsel offer excuses for his behaviour (as he does at the end of the scene) and the prosecuting counsel lists Tseng's crimes and argues why the punishments are appropriate. Both the defence and the prosecution could call witnesses (such as the banished courtiers, for example, or Ping-wur).

Scene 5

When the lights go up, we can still hear the bubbling sound, but it is low now, such as a pot of soup might make upon an open fire. And that, indeed, is what it is. TSENG lies on the floor of the OLD MAN's hut, gently whimpering, and the OLD MAN himself is calmly and silently stirring his simmering supper.

TSENG *(Still half asleep.)* No! That awful noise! Take it away! I'll be a better person! Give me another chance, another . . . *(Waking up.)* another . . .

(He sits up and immediately flinches at the bubbling sound. Then, reassured that he is no longer in hell, looks around, bewildered. He stands and walks slowly round the hut, touching the walls as if to check that everything is real. Finally he approaches the OLD MAN, who has taken no notice of him, but continues to stir the bubbling pot.)

How long have I been . . . ?

(He walks away again, clearly struggling to puzzle it all out.)

So it was all . . . ? I was never in hell at all . . . No boiling oil . . . *(He laughs and runs back to the OLD MAN, pointing at the pot.)* Yes! It was your stupid soup! I must have heard it bubbling in my dream. That's it! I drank a bowlful, didn't I, before dozing off. The foul stuff probably gave me indigestion. They say that causes nightmares. So I was never banished at all, never killed by robbers . . . *(The greatest realisation of all.)* And never High Chamberlain!

(There is another silence as TSENG thinks about his dream. He is plainly weighing things up and coming to a decision. It could go either way, and now the OLD MAN is watching him, his expression a mixture of hope and fear . . .)

But I **could** be High Chamberlain!

(The OLD MAN sinks his head in disappointment and stops stirring the soup.)

I could be if I tried! They say that dreams speak the truth. If that's so, I've learned a lot. I know the ropes now; it wouldn't be difficult to worm my way in . . . Some fairly low-level job at first, but then, bit by bit, a little bribery here, a little blackmail there . . . Oh, yes, I will be High Chamberlain Tseng once more! *(He stops and thinks.)* No. Not once more: for the first time. All that other stuff was a dream! *(He goes up to the OLD MAN again and shouts in his face.)* A stupid dream, old man, brought on by your disgusting soup! *(He goes to the door and turns back.)* A useful dream, though. I've learned a very handy lesson!

(TSENG laughs, but, as he takes hold of the latch on the door, he is stopped by the sound of voices outside. At first they are indistinct, but soon we pick up the words 'Oranges! Fresh oranges for sale!' The OLD MAN watches TSENG, as the colour drains from his face and he backs away from the door.)

Oranges . . . ? Why do those voices send a chill down my spine?

(The shouts grow louder until, with a sharp rap on the door, the owners of the voices enter, pushing a small barrow with a painted board along the side which reads: 'LING and YAMMO. Fruiterers to the nobility. Service with a smile and a witty quip'. TSENG points at them in amazement . . .)

I've seen you before . . . You . . . You were . . .

(LING and YAMMO look at each other and then back to him, in puzzlement, as he staggers past them to the door.)

All right . . . I give in . . . I think I understand now . . .

THE TESTING OF TSENG — SCENE 5

LING	*(Still puzzled by the stranger's reaction.)* Sorry. Were we interrupting something? 60
YAMMO	Please don't go on our account.
	(But TSENG takes one last look around the room, his eyes wild with fear, bows respectfully to the OLD MAN, and leaves.)
	Funny bloke. Anyway, back to business. *(He shouts, as though still in the street.)* Oranges! Fresh oranges for sale! Or . . .
	(LING takes him by the arm and leads him to one side.)
LING	Looking at the thinness of that soup, I don't think we're going to make much of a sale here, Yammo. 70
YAMMO	Oh . . . Right . . . Shall I just . . . ?
	(LING nods. YAMMO takes an orange from the barrow, dusts it off on the seat of his trousers and presents it to the OLD MAN.)
	Compliments of Ling and Yammo, fruiterers to the . . . et cetera.
	(The OLD MAN takes the orange and bows to YAMMO, who bows back.)
LING	*(Who has been looking through the open doorway.)* Are you expecting a visitor, old man? Young chap? Looks a bit cocky? 80
	(The OLD MAN nods, smiles and sits down cross-legged on the mat.)

 **et cetera** *And so on. (An expression used in order to avoid having to repeat a list or long sentence.)*

YAMMO	*(Looks at LING and shrugs.)* Well . . . We'll be off then . . .
	(They exit and we hear the cries of 'Oranges! Fresh oranges . . . !' receding into the distance. There is a brief silence and then the sound of approaching footsteps. They stop and a young man's voice is heard, bad-tempered and arrogant.)
YOUNG MAN	What a place for your horse to go lame! And there's a storm brewing. I say! Within there!
	(He strides into the hut. He is dressed well and knows it.)
	What's the matter with you? Didn't you hear me call? *(He looks at the OLD MAN.)* Hm! Deaf, blind or merely stupid, I wonder. Ah! Soup . . . !
	He approaches the pot and helps himself to some soup. The OLD MAN smiles once more and, as the lights dim, we hear a distant peal of thunder . . .

90

DISCUSSION: Hold a class discussion about the ending of the play.
1. What does the stage direction mean by 'It could go either way' and why might the old man be watching Tseng at that moment in 'a mixture of hope and fear' (lines 24–25)?
2. Why does the colour drain from Tseng's face as he hears the cries of 'Oranges!'?
3. Why does Tseng say 'I think I understand now'? What does he understand? What has he learned from the experience?
4. Why, after being so insolent earlier, does Tseng now bow respectfully to the old man before he leaves?
5. In what ways might Tseng be a better person in future?
6. What do you think is going to happen to the young man who enters at the end? Why does the old man smile as the lights dim?
7. Who is the old man? What power does he seem to possess?

WRITING: As the play ends, another arrogant young man arrives in the hut. What would happen if the play were to carry on, instead of ending here? Write the first scene of a continuation, in which the new arrival behaves badly (but in different ways from Tseng), and drinks the soup.

DISCUSSION: One interpretation of the ending is that Tseng is about to return to his old arrogant and unscrupulous ways, and is only stopped by the realisation that his memory of being killed and meeting the Emperor of the Dead might not have been a dream after all. Does the play seem to suggest that it is only the threat of hell and eternal torture that keeps us on the straight and narrow path? Is it that Tseng has not reformed at all; but simply resolves to be a better person because of the fear of worse punishment?

Dramascripts

The Question

Dramatised by
JOHN O'CONNOR

Where the tale comes from

The Question is based upon two traditional stories which the poet Geoffrey Chaucer first brought together in the fourteenth century as *The Wife of Bath's Tale*.

Based in the court of King Arthur, and featuring knights, quests and magic, the play's origins lie in medieval England, Wales and France; but, such is the relevance of the issues which these ancient tales raise, that they might have been composed yesterday.

NELSON DRAMASCRIPTS

THE CHARACTERS

(in order of appearance)

QUEEN GUINEVERE

KING ARTHUR

ALISON

THE KNIGHT

OTHER KNIGHTS, LADIES, COURTIERS*

1ST WOMAN

2ND WOMAN

3RD WOMAN

4TH WOMAN

OLD WOMAN

OTHER WOMEN ENCOUNTERED ON THE KNIGHT'S TRAVELS*

* *indicates non-speaking part*

THE QUESTION

SCENE 1

A hall in Camelot. QUEEN GUINEVERE sits alone, serious and deep in thought. She stirs as a distant fanfare is heard and stands as her husband enters the room.

GUINEVERE	What was the sentence?	1
ARTHUR	Guilty. He's to be executed tomorrow.	
	(She does not reply. Assuming that her silence means that she disapproves, ARTHUR goes on, justifying his judgement.)	
	He used his power as a knight to violate a young woman – you wouldn't have him go unpunished, Guinevere?	
GUINEVERE	Of course not.	
ARTHUR	I know it's a waste. I feel that as much as you do.	10
GUINEVERE	It's not that . . . This is his first crime, isn't it?	
ARTHUR	Yes, but that is hardly the point. If we were talking about theft or . . . or bribery, I could simply strip him of his title and throw him into prison for a while. But this. I have no alternative.	

Camelot King Arthur's castle, traditionally situated somewhere in the west of England.

violate Rape.

SCENE 1

GUINEVERE	Alison has an alternative.
ARTHUR	What do you mean?
GUINEVERE	I have just spoken to her. She came to me – of her own free will; I didn't send for her.
ARTHUR	To plead on his behalf? His victim?
GUINEVERE	To ask for a different sentence.
ARTHUR	What does she have in mind?
	(GUINEVERE pauses, thinking carefully.)
GUINEVERE	As supreme head of the courts, you have of course every right to do with this young man as you wish. But there is an ancient statute – I don't think it has been invoked for many years – which permits the Queen and her women to pass judgement on crimes which are enacted against her women, as this surely was.
ARTHUR	And you wish to sentence him yourself?
GUINEVERE	On Alison's advice. Yes.
ARTHUR	Do you have it in mind to set him free?
GUINEVERE	No. Simply to find a different way in which to punish him.
	(ARTHUR looks at her, pauses for a moment and then smiles.)
ARTHUR	Re-convene the court. I cannot wait to hear this sentence.

statute *Written law.*

invoked *Called upon to be used.*

Re-convene *Call to assembly again.*

THE QUESTION SCENE 1

(GUINEVERE nods to a servant, who exits. We hear the sound of a fanfare. Instantly the stage is full of COURTIERS, who take their places as though in a court of law, the knights on ARTHUR's side, the ladies on GUINEVERE's. A young man then enters from the left between two soldiers, and kneels before the KING and QUEEN, his head bowed. ALISON herself enters from the right, and is offered the seat next to GUINEVERE. The QUEEN and ALISON confer briefly and the court falls silent.)

GUINEVERE Sir knight. You have been found guilty and are sentenced to suffer the punishment of death. Following the ancient statutes, however, you are now in my power. Hear your new sentence.

(In shock, he looks up.)

You will leave this court a free man *(There is a sense of shock in the court, but no-one is bold enough to say anything.)*, but will remain free on one condition only: that you return in a year and a day, at which time you will give the answer to a question that I am about to set you. If in the judgement of my women and myself you answer satisfactorily, you will be free for ever. If you cannot answer, or give an answer which does not please us, your head will be struck from your shoulders. Is that clear?

KNIGHT *(Whispers.)* Yes, your majesty.

GUINEVERE Do you give your word to return on the day assigned?

KNIGHT I give my word, your majesty.

GUINEVERE Then the question is a simple one, and it is this. What is it that women most desire?

There is a stunned silence, but clearly the court approves of the new sentence. Then, still noiselessly, GUINEVERE and ARTHUR stand and leave the room, followed by the whole court except the KNIGHT himself. Up to now still in his kneeling position, he collapses on the floor, as though exhausted. As the lights dim, he slowly hauls himself to his feet, straightens his clothes and leaves the court to begin his quest.

DISCUSSION: Brainstorm everything you know about King Arthur and the Knights of the Round Table. How were they expected to behave towards other people?

ARTWORK: Work out a design for the staging of the court scene and draw a rough sketch of it. Then decide where the courtiers might stand or sit and where Arthur, Guinevere, Alison and the knight might be placed, and add them to your sketch. Write notes around the sketch to explain why you have chosen to place characters in particular positions.

WRITING: Write Guinevere's diary for the night after the knight's trial. Give her views on why the new sentence imposed on the knight seems to be an appropriate one, and why Alison might have advised her to change the original sentence.

Scene 2

After a few seconds of music, the lights come up on a balcony above the stage. ARTHUR is studying a map and GUINEVERE reading a letter.

ARTHUR	So he is still somewhere in Wessex.	1
GUINEVERE	Scouring the countryside. Asking every woman he meets what it is that women most desire. *(She smiles.)*	
ARTHUR	*(Pinning the map of England to the back wall.)* You seem amused.	
GUINEVERE	I was just thinking of some of the strange responses he must be getting.	
	The lights dim quickly on the balcony and come up on the stage below. The next line of dialogue should follow immediately upon GUINEVERE's.	

Wessex The ancient kingdom covering the west of England and parts of the south.

Scene 3

The sounds of carts trundling and voices of market people indicate that we are in a busy village somewhere. The KNIGHT, now in travelling clothes and carrying a leather bag, is talking to THREE WOMEN and writing down their responses on a scroll.

1ST WOMAN	Chocolate.
KNIGHT	Chocolate?
1ST WOMAN	Women most desire chocolate.
2ND WOMAN	Nice clothes for me.
	(A 4th WOMAN enters.)

4TH WOMAN	Is this a survey?
KNIGHT	Not exactly. Sort of research.
3RD WOMAN	You ought to set up a focus group.
KNIGHT	A what?
3RD WOMAN	Get loads of women together and put it to the vote.
KNIGHT	I somehow don't think that's the way I'm supposed to go about it.
4TH WOMAN	This is a kind of job then, is it? A quest? A mission?
KNIGHT	Yes.
4TH WOMAN	Who are you working for?
KNIGHT	Myself, I suppose.
4TH WOMAN	I mean, who set you the task?
KNIGHT	*(He pauses before answering.)* Queen Guinevere actually.
	(There is general amazement.)
4TH WOMAN	Why? *(Suspiciously.)* Something you'd done?
KNIGHT	Something I'd done, yes.
	The lights dim on the stage and come up on the balcony.

 **focus group** *A collection of people who are brought together to give their opinions on something.*

Scene 4

Brief music, to suggest the passage of time. ARTHUR and GUINEVERE are still on the balcony, and ARTHUR is drawing the line of the KNIGHT's route on the map which he pinned to the wall earlier. He has reached the Midlands.

ARTHUR	Mercia.	1
GUINEVERE	He's certainly covering some ground.	
ARTHUR	How long has he been away now?	
GUINEVERE	It's the end of March.	
ARTHUR	So: nearly four months.	
GUINEVERE	And what is he learning, I wonder?	
	Brief music, as lights dim on the balcony and come up on the stage.	

Scene 5

The KNIGHT is sitting disconsolately on the ground, trying to make sense of the information that he has acquired. He has plainly written every response down on his scroll, which now stretches half way across the stage.

KNIGHT This is impossible! There have hardly been any two women who have given me the same answer. What do women most desire? Well, according to the women of Wessex, Mercia and Northumbria . . . *(He reads a few sample responses, rolling up the scroll as he goes through the list.)*: women most desire . . . wealth, high society, eternal beauty . . . *(His voice drops in embarrassment.)* an enjoyable sex life . . . *(He reads on quickly.)* cheap wine . . . amazing how many want 'to be happy and travel' . . . some like to be flattered . . . *(He reads one, word for word.)* 'Women most desire to be trusted' . . . hmmm, fair enough . . . *(Scanning the final yard of the scroll.)* and a significant proportion refuse to answer on the grounds that it's gender stereotyping . . .

(There is a clap of thunder and we hear the sound of rain falling.)

That's all I need.

(He pulls his cloak around him, picks up the bag and hoists it on to his shoulder.)

disconsolately Miserably; unable to be cheered up.

Mercia and Northumbria The ancient kingdoms covering, respectively, the midland and northern counties of England.

gender stereotyping Assuming that women (or men) behave in typical ways.

Ah well, on to York, I suppose . . .

Slowly and dispiritedly he leaves the stage as another, louder clap of thunder fills the air, the lights dim and the rain can be heard falling in torrents.

SCENE 6

The following dumb-show is accompanied by music. On the balcony, ARTHUR and GUINEVERE enter; GUINEVERE reads from a letter (presumably a report on the KNIGHT's travels) and ARTHUR marks the route on the map pinned to the wall. Cross-fade to the stage, where the KNIGHT is questioning more women and writing down their responses on his ever-lengthening scroll. For a short while women enter, talk to the KNIGHT and depart. Then cross-fade back to the balcony, where GUINEVERE is marking in the KNIGHT's continuing travels. Cross-fade back to the stage to see more of the KNIGHT's interviewing . . .

This repeated cross-fading should not go on so long as to bore the audience, but should be enough to represent the KNIGHT's travels and the passage of time. By the end of the sequence, the line on the map should have zig-zagged all over England and be returning to the West Country.

dumb-show *A scene acted without words.*

Cross-fade *As the lights dim on one part of the stage, they come up on another.*

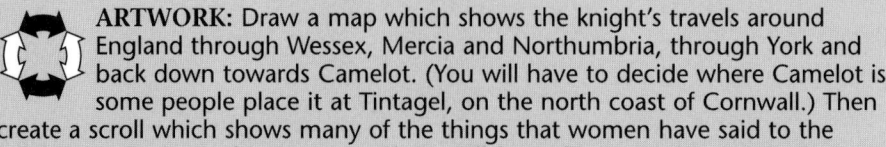 **ARTWORK:** Draw a map which shows the knight's travels around England through Wessex, Mercia and Northumbria, through York and back down towards Camelot. (You will have to decide where Camelot is: some people place it at Tintagel, on the north coast of Cornwall.) Then create a scroll which shows many of the things that women have said to the knight in response to his question. These will form the basis of a wall display.

IMPROVISATION: In groups of eight, improvise the actions of Scene 6, bringing out the knight's increasing exhaustion and despondency and the contrastingly lively reactions of the woman he speaks to. Arrange the acting area so that Arthur and Guinevere can be seen performing their actions of marking the map. It will help to have some music playing in the background: decide what you think would be most appropriate.

WRITING: Write three entries in the knight's diary. The first could be just after he leaves the court; the second could be after a few weeks of his quest; and the third at the point where he sets off for York. Show his initial anxieties and the way in which he begins to feel that he will never find the answer.

DISCUSSION: Look back at the answers that different women have offered in response to the question 'What is it that women most desire?'. Then hold a class discussion based on the following questions: (a) What would your own answer be? (b) What answer do you think would best fit the story?

Scene 7

As the women disperse for the last time, the KNIGHT drops his scroll in despair.

KNIGHT Oh, I don't know. The answer could be any of these – how am I to know? Perhaps there isn't an answer at all. Perhaps this is just some trick to punish me. *(His nerve is beginning to fail him.)* Perhaps if I were to head off back to Scotland and hide myself in the hills . . .

(Almost convinced that this is the only sensible plan, he is backing off stage, left, and has not seen an OLD WOMAN behind him. She is toothless, dressed in rags and bent over with age.)

OLD WOMAN That's not the way, young man.

KNIGHT What?

OLD WOMAN That's not the way.

KNIGHT *(Suffering from stress, he has become extremely short-tempered.)* But you don't know where I want to go, old woman.

OLD WOMAN You want the answer to a question.

KNIGHT *(Surprised; then he realises that she must have been around earlier.)* Oh, you've been listening, have you?

OLD WOMAN I know the answer. Any fool could tell you the answer. You even know it yourself, if only you'd think.

KNIGHT *(He feels that he ought to scoff, but there is something about her that prevents him.)* Are you a witch?

(She doesn't answer.)

OLD WOMAN In seven days you must stand before Guinevere's court and tell her what it is that women most desire. If you cannot tell, or give an answer which does not satisfy, your head will be removed from your shoulders. *(He is now in her power and simply stands staring at her.)* I will be there by your side. I will whisper the answer in your ear and you will be free. The only reward I ask is that you will do the next thing I require of you. Is it a bargain between us?

He nods dumbly. She smiles and hobbles off as the lights dim on the motionless and bewildered KNIGHT.

Scene 8

A fanfare signals that we are once again in KING ARTHUR's court. As before, the courtiers take their places, with ARTHUR and GUINEVERE entering after them, the QUEEN accompanied by ALISON. The KNIGHT enters last and stands before GUINEVERE. He is shaking and sweating with fear: the OLD WOMAN is nowhere to be seen.

GUINEVERE	Sir knight, it is a year and a day since you departed from this court on a quest to find the answer to the question 'What is it that women most desire?' Are you ready to give your answer?
	(He anxiously looks around for the OLD WOMAN, but to no avail. Turning to the QUEEN, he prepares to offer the best answer that he can think of from the many hundreds that have been offered to him.)
KNIGHT	Your majesty, women most desire . . . they most desire . . .
	(He closes his eyes and takes a deep breath. When he opens them, the OLD WOMAN is standing next to him. She whispers in his ear and he delivers his answer.)
	Women most desire . . . to have power.
	(There is a tense silence: has he given the right answer?)
GUINEVERE	Go on.
KNIGHT	They desire not to have to follow men's wishes all the time . . .
GUINEVERE	And?
KNIGHT	And not to have men forcing them to do things against their will . . .

SCENE 8

(Silence. Then GUINEVERE stands and the rest of the court rise with her.)

GUINEVERE Good. Remember that.

(Silently and seriously, GUINEVERE, ARTHUR and the court disperse. The KNIGHT collapses in relief and exhaustion. Then he drags himself to his feet and is about to leave the court when he is stopped by the voice of the OLD WOMAN.)

OLD WOMAN Haven't you forgotten something?

KNIGHT Oh. Sorry.

(He reaches into his pocket and offers her a bag of gold.)

OLD WOMAN Something else.

KNIGHT *(He thinks and then realises.)* Oh . . . Thank you. You saved my life: thank you.

OLD WOMAN We had a bargain.

KNIGHT Did we?

OLD WOMAN You are to do the next thing I require of you.

KNIGHT Oh. I'd forgotten. Well? What can I do for you? What do you want?

OLD WOMAN I want you to marry me.

(He roars with laughter. In his relief at escaping with his life, he is a little hysterical.)

KNIGHT Very good, old woman, very good. But seriously, though. You must have some reward: what do you want?

 **hysterical** His emotions are almost out of control.

THE QUESTION SCENE 8

OLD WOMAN I've told you. I want you as my husband.

GUINEVERE *(Who has re-entered silently.)* And if it was a bargain, it has to be kept . . . Wouldn't you say?

As he turns to look at GUINEVERE and then back at the OLD WOMAN, his expression shows his sudden realisation that this is all horribly real . . . 50

Scene 9

The KNIGHT and the OLD WOMAN are in an enormous double bed. She is wearing nothing but a rather nasty-looking nightdress, while he is fully clothed; she is smiling seductively at him in her toothless way: he is staring straight ahead, eyes bulging in sheer revulsion.

OLD WOMAN *(Leaning over to his side of the bed.)* Well, come on then. This is our wedding night, after all. *(She snuggles up more closely.)* I thought you Knights of the Round Table had a reputation as great lovers. *(She moves even closer.)* What's made you so coy?

(Unable to stand any more, he leaps out of the bed, draws his sword and points it at her.)

KNIGHT Don't come any closer – I'm warning you!

THE QUESTION — SCENE 9

OLD WOMAN	What have I done? *(Smiling winningly – in other words, flashing her gums at him.)* You don't have to be shy of me. I'm your little wife!
KNIGHT	Oh no you're not!
OLD WOMAN	Yes I am: we were married this morning, don't you remember? And the Queen made a public declaration that, if you weren't a proper husband to me . . . If you didn't fulfil all the duties expected of a husband . . . She would carry out the death sentence hanging over you.
KNIGHT	*(Groaning in despair.)* I know, I know.
OLD WOMAN	So what's your problem? You can tell me.
KNIGHT	Problem? *(Shouting hysterically.)* Problem! I'll tell you what my problem is, since you ask. My problem is that you are old; my problem is that you are ugly; and to make matters worse, you are seriously working-class!
OLD WOMAN	Ah, so that's all.
KNIGHT	All?
	(He groans and sits on the floor. She watches him for a moment, smiling to herself.)
OLD WOMAN	Let's just think for a moment about what you've just said. You complain that I am old. But surely you have been taught to respect age? The old are wise and experienced, not subject to wild flights of fancy or irresponsibility. You say I'm ugly. So much the better:

 **working-class** *The knight snobbishly rejects the old woman because he views her as coming from the lowest rank of society.*

SCENE 9

you won't have to worry that all the handsome young men of the neighbourhood will be dropping in to see me while you're away on quests or righting wrongs in distant parts of the kingdom. And as for being low-born . . . I had always been brought up to believe that true nobility wasn't something that you could inherit in a will, like a grand title or rich estates. *(He looks up: she has touched a nerve.)* True nobility is all about the way we behave to other people; it's about sympathy and compassion, generosity and open-heartedness, tolerance and understanding . . . Respect for the feelings of others . . . *(He hangs his head in shame.)* Am I making sense?

KNIGHT Yes, you are. Great sense.

(He stands, turns to her and bows.)

I beg you to forgive me for my insulting words. I am sincerely sorry for the way I have behaved to you.

(She looks at him steadily.)

OLD WOMAN Yes, I believe you are. Come and sit by me.

(He sits on the edge of the bed and looks at her.)

I could make everything better, you know: I could solve all your problems.

KNIGHT I don't understand.

OLD WOMAN I am going to offer you a choice.

KNIGHT A choice?

OLD WOMAN Yes, and it is this. Either you can have a wife who is young and beautiful – but take your chance about what might happen with all the good-looking young men who will call in while you're away . . . Or have me as I am: old and ugly – but devoted to you and ever faithful . . .

(She pauses to let the implications of the alternatives sink in.)

Now, which is it to be? Choose. But I warn you that you will have to live with your choice until the day you die.

(He stands up in a confused daze. Then he paces around the room. At one point he seems to come to a decision.)

KNIGHT   I want you to be . . .

(And then instantly changes his mind.)

No. What I want is . . .

(But that choice is even more disturbing. Staring around the room for inspiration, he meets her gaze, and in that instant he seems to see things clearly for the first time . . . When he speaks, it is slowly and with great conviction.)

Dear wife, you choose for us both. I will accept whatever you think is right.

OLD WOMAN   You put yourself in my power?

KNIGHT   Totally.

(As he utters the word, there is a lightning flash, a massive peal of thunder and a momentary blackout. In bed sits a beautiful young woman.)

ALISON   Then kiss me, husband, for I will give you the best of both worlds: I will be both young and faithful. *(He tries to speak.)* Ask nothing. Little by little you will understand . . . In fact, unless I am mistaken, you have begun to understand already.

The lights dim as they embrace.

ARTWORK AND WRITING: Draw your impression of the old woman, based upon the details provided in the script and the way the knight reacts to having to marry her. Then write a full description of her, which could be added to the stage directions when she first appears in Scene 7.

ARTWORK: Imagine you were filming this story. Draw four key frames to represent different moments in Scene 9.

LANGUAGE: Although the play is set in the days of King Arthur, the language is modern and there are also references to things which could only exist in the twentieth century (such as 'focus-groups' on page 73). When a writer includes an expression or an event which seems to be from the wrong period in history, we call it an anachronism (from ancient Greek words meaning 'out-of-time-ness'). One striking anachronism is the knight's use of the expression 'working-class' (page 85). Does this seem to be completely out of place? Why do you think the writer might have chosen this expression rather than something more appropriate to the medieval period, such as 'low-born', for example?

DISCUSSION: Hold a class discussion on whether you think the knight's punishment fitted his crime. First answer the following questions:
1. What was his crime?
2. What was Guinevere's sentence, after listening to Alison's advice?
3. How was he punished by having to carry out that sentence?
4. Why was that punishment appropriate for the crime he committed?
5. Why did Guinevere approve of the answer he gave in court (that women most desire power)?
6. The knight receives a second punishment when he has to marry the old woman. Why is that particularly appropriate?
7. As the play ends, Alison says, '...unless I am mistaken, you have begun to understand already.' What has the knight begun to understand? What lessons should he have learned?

HOT-SEATING: Hot-seat the knight and question him about his experiences. Among other things, you might ask what he has learned since the sentence of death was passed upon him and Queen Guinevere commuted it to a quest. What effect did it have, being forced to question thousands of women on what women most desire, knowing that his life depended upon finding an answer that would satisfy the women of the court? What did he learn from the old woman's behaviour towards him and what she said on their wedding night?

WRITING: Write a letter from Alison to Queen Guinevere, in which she gives her views on (a) whether she feels the knight has been sufficiently punished for his crime; and (b) what she thinks he might have learned from the punishments.

Looking Back at the Plays

1 **Discussion: casting the roles**
   In pairs, pick one of the plays and discuss which film or television actors you would cast in each of the roles, noting down brief reasons to support your choices. Compare your ideas in a class discussion.

2 **Artwork and writing: designing a poster**
   Work in pairs to design a poster advertising a stage, television or film version of one of the plays. First discuss as a class the words and images that usually appear on a poster of this kind.

3 **Artwork and writing: a theatre programme**
   Create a programme for a theatre performance, either of one of the plays, or for a production in which all three would be put on together (a 'triple bill'). Remember to include a cast that you have decided on, as well as any illustrations that would be helpful to the audience.

4 **Discussion and writing: a review**
   Which of the three plays did you enjoy most?
   For each play, discuss features such as the plots, the characters, the dialogue, the setting and the level of excitement or mystery. Then write a review of the play you considered to be the best.

5 **Writing a story: a story of crime and punishment**
   Write a story or a play in which someone commits a crime and is then given a punishment which (a) fits the crime; and (b) enables him or her to learn from what they have done.

6 **Discussion and writing: ten years on**
   Discuss what each of the following might be doing ten years after the ends of their stories: Carl; Tseng; and either Alison or the knight. Then write a letter from the character to a friend, explaining how the events of ten years earlier have changed them.

LOOKING BACK AT THE PLAYS

7 WRITING: A RADIO PLAY

Each of the three plays could work very well on radio. Select one of the following extracts and (a) list the sound effects and music which might be required; and (b) redraft the section for radio: Scenes 9 and 10 of *Lad Carl*; Scenes 3 and 4 of *The Testing of Tseng*; or Scene 9 of *The Question*.

8 ARTWORK: CREATING A DISPLAY

Create a classroom display to represent the three plays. You could include:
- brief summaries of the three plays;
- artwork, such as: the storyboard frames, designs for staging and costume, newspaper reports, timelines, impressions of characters and props (such as the map showing the knight's travels and the scroll containing the women's answers to his question);
- the posters and theatre programmes created for activities 2 and 3 above.

9 DISCUSSION: CRIME AND PUNISHMENT

Some people argue that wrongdoers should be punished severely, so that (a) they will be deterred from repeating their crime; and (b) others will be deterred too. Others argue that the most important thing is that wrongdoers should be made to think about what they have done and should be given a punishment which will help them to reform and become law-abiding citizens. Use evidence from the three plays, as well as your own knowledge of the world around you, to decide whether you are more inclined to support (a) or (b). Then hold a class discussion in which you share your views with others.